SHADOW
SQUADRON

DARK AGENT

ZD13.671

Raintree

SHADOW SQUADRON

DARK AGENT

WRITTEN BY
CARL BOWEN

ILLUSTRATED BY
WILSON TORTOSA

AND
BENNY FUENTES

2012.241

Raintree is an imprint of Capstone Global Library
Limited, a company incorporated in England and
Wales having its registered office at 7 Pilgrim
Street, London, EC4V 6LB Registered company
number: 6695582

www.raintreepublishers.co.uk
myorders@raintreepublishers.co.uk

First published by Stone Arch Books © 2015
First published in the United Kingdom in 2015

The moral rights of the proprietor have been
asserted.

Designed by Brann Garvey

ISBN: 978- 1-406-28570-3 (paperback)
19 18 17 16 15
10 9 8 7 6 5 4 3 2 1

British Library Cataloguing in Publication Data
A full catalogue record for this book is available
from the British Library.

Printed in China by Nordica
0414/CA21400598

CONTENTS

ACCESS GRANTED

2012.101

CLASSIFIED

SHADOW SQUADRON DOSSIER

CROSS, RYAN

RANK: Lieutenant Commander
BRANCH: Navy SEAL
PSYCH PROFILE: Cross is the
team leader of Shadow Squadron.
Control oriented and loyal, Cross
insisted on hand-picking each
member of his squad.

WALKER, ALONSO

RANK: Chief Petty Officer
BRANCH: Navy SEAL
PSYCH PROFILE: Walker is Shadow
Squadron's second-in-command.
His combat experience, skepticism,
and distrustful nature make him a
good counter-balance to Cross's
leadership.

YAMASHITA, KIMIYO

RANK: Lieutenant
BRANCH: Army Ranger
PSYCH PROFILE: The team's sniper is
an expert marksman and a true stoic.
It seems his emotions are as steady
as his trigger finger.

LANCASTER, MORGAN

RANK: Staff Sergeant
BRANCH: Air Force Combat Control
PSYCH PROFILE: The team's newest member is a tech expert who learns fast and has the ability to adapt to any combat situation.

JANNATI, ARAM

RANK: Second Lieutenant
BRANCH: Army Ranger
PSYCH PROFILE: Jannati serves as the team's linguist. His sharp eyes serve him well as a spotter, and he's usually paired with Yamashita on overwatch.

PHOTO NOT AVAILABLE

SHEPHERD, MARK

RANK: Lieutenant
BRANCH: Army (Green Beret)
PSYCH PROFILE: The heavy-weapons expert of the group, Shepherd's love of combat borders on unhealthy.

PHOTO NOT AVAILABLE

MISSION BRIEFING

OPERATION

DARK AGENT 5678

CIA agent Bradley Upton has intel to share with us regarding a particularly dangerous bomb maker nicknamed "the Professor." I've had a few close calls with him in the past, so let's just say I want us to be entirely committed to capturing him once and for all.

We'll head to Yemen immediately and begin setting up a snare to catch this elusive explosives expert.

— Lieutenant Commander Ryan Cross

3245.98 ● ● ●

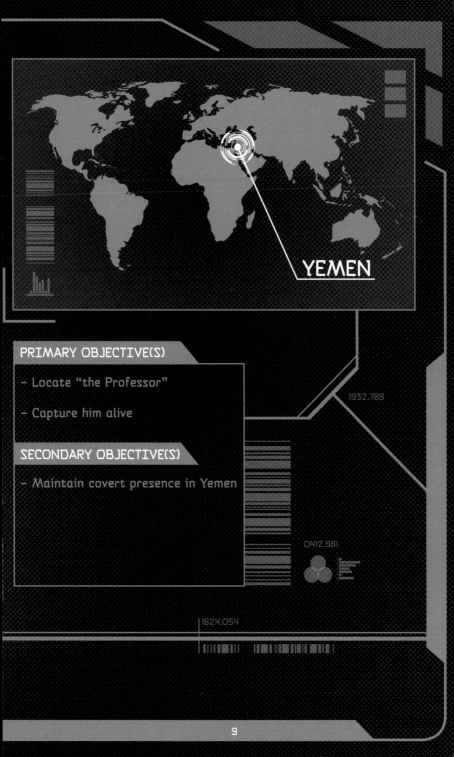

YEMEN

PRIMARY OBJECTIVE(S)

- Locate "the Professor"

- Capture him alive

SECONDARY OBJECTIVE(S)

- Maintain covert presence in Yemen

1932.789

0412.981

1624.054

INTEL

DECRYPTING

12345

COM CHATTER

- BALLISTIC VEST: chest armour capable of resisting the impact of some bullets

- CANALPHONE: radio earpiece that fits inside the ear canal

- SIG P226: a full-sized, high capacity pistol

- ZIP TIE: a plastic, adjustable strap used as handcuffs in the field

3245.98 ● ● ●

THE PROFESSOR

Somewhere in Yemen . . .

SPLASH!

A burst of frigid water splashed into Lieutenant Commander Ryan Cross's face, returning him to consciousness and stealing his breath. He coughed and tried to spit water out of his mouth and nose. His confused mind struggled to fight the fear that he was drowning. *Dying.*

The terror passed only after he'd gagged and sneezed out the last bit of water. When he opened his eyes, he saw that he had a new reason to fear for his life. Standing before him was a nightmare from Cross's past. The man held an empty, dripping bucket in his hands.

The man leered at Cross with a twisted mix of delight and hatred. "We've never met," the man said. He spoke in English with an Arabic accent. "And I'd been pleased by that fact. Your reputation precedes you. But now that I have you face-to-face . . . I don't find you all that fearsome."

Cross had to admit that he didn't feel particularly fearsome at that moment. He had been drugged and beaten. His face was a mask of pain, and his left eye was nearly swollen shut. The canalphone he usually wore nestled in his left ear was gone. He still wore the civilian clothes he'd been wearing when he was taken, but his SIG P226 pistol, his utility knife, and his ballistic vest were all gone. It was the loss of the canalphone that troubled him the most. Without it, he couldn't hear or talk to his team.

Cross's first attempt to speak ended in a retching cough, and he spat up one last spray of water.

"You are lost," Cross's captor said. He was a Middle Eastern man with a scraggly beard and thinning hair. He wore pince-nez glasses, but his dark, beady eyes were visible. The teeth that showed through his sick smile were long and crooked and more yellow than white. Although the face was familiar to Cross, he didn't know the man's real name.

"All the same," the man continued, "a chance at freedom yet remains for you. Perhaps even heroism."

The man stepped back to set aside the bucket. Cross took a look at his surroundings. He was bound to a metal desk chair with plastic zip-ties around both ankles and his left wrist. A nylon rope bound his thighs to the seat. For some reason, his right arm was free.

A glance around revealed that he was in a windowless interior room. A leather couch was opposite him. A wooden coffee table with a glass top was between them. Bookshelves and standing lamps lined one wall. A brown, red, and yellow carpet lay beneath the coffee table.

The man had moved to the threshold of the open door to Cross's right, which Cross noted was the only way out. "Bring him in," the man said.

Someone outside answered. A moment later, a hunched and hooded figure was shoved into the room. Cross's captor took charge of this second prisoner. The man bound the prisoner's wrists with nylon cord then shut the door behind him. He led the hooded man to the couch and shoved him down. Cross recognized the prisoner's clothing.

"Here lies the gateway to your freedom," their captor said, turning back to Cross. As he spoke, he produced Cross's SIG P226 from beneath his robe and laid it on the coffee table, close to Cross's side. "You need only raise this gun and shoot this man, and you will be free."

"Or I could shoot you," Cross croaked. "Might be worth it."

"Satisfying to your ego, perhaps," the man said, "but a waste of both our lives. We are not alone here. If your gunshot is not followed immediately by word from me, those who wait outside will come in and kill you both. And you have only one bullet. Enough for him, or for me. But I think you will find killing this one rewarding. For if you kill him, not only will I let you live, but I will turn myself in as well. I will submit myself to American justice, whatever form

it takes. The only price is this man's life. Will you pay it?"

"Who is he?" Cross asked, trying to stall.

A malevolent smile twisted the man's face. "I should make you decide before I answer that," the man said. "I am not so cruel, however."

He lifted the stiff burlap hood from the prisoner's face. The man beneath was just as bruised and bloody as Cross felt. The left lens of his John Lennon glasses was cracked, and the frame sat crooked on his bleeding nose. He lifted his head, and his eyes met Cross's gaze.

"Ryan," he choked out.

"Agent Upton," Cross said. "Didn't I tell you to stay in the van?"

A weak smile rose to Upton's lips. "I had to pee."

* * *

One Week Earlier . . .

Cross rubbed his right forearm as he entered the briefing room of Shadow Squadron's headquarters.

The room was already full when Cross arrived. He saw his second-in-command, Chief Petty Officer Alonso Walker, hunched over Cross's spot at the head of the conference table. He was operating the computer touchpad recessed into the table's surface. At Walker's command, the globe-and-crossed-swords emblem of Joint Special Operations Command bloomed on the computer whiteboard behind him.

Cross normally set up the briefing equipment before a meeting, but last-minute communications with Command and a painful shot in the arm from the base's doctor had delayed him. Fortunately, Walker had taken the initiative in Cross's absence.

A year ago, Walker's initiative might have agitated the Commander. When he'd left the Navy SEALs to join Shadow Squadron, Cross had got plenty of static from the Chief. Walker had been second-in-command on his previous team. When his superior had been killed in action, Walker had expected to take the lead in his place. Instead, the brass at JSOC recruited Cross to fill the leadership spot on a new team — Shadow Squadron — with Walker as his second.

It had been a long, hard road breaking the Chief of the habit of trying to subvert Cross's authority. Harder still had been convincing the older soldier that Cross was the better man for the job.

Months of intense training and a long list of successful missions had eventually earned Walker's respect. They'd since forged a bond of brotherhood between them. Cross counted their friendship as one of his greatest accomplishments.

Of course, the successful missions were nothing to dismiss. Shadow Squadron was a top-secret eight-soldier special-missions team assembled from elite soldiers from all branches of the US military. The team included members from the Navy SEALs, Green Berets, Army Rangers, Air Force Combat Control, and Marine Special Operations Regiment. The team travelled all over the world to root out terrorist threats, hunt criminals, rescue hostages, defend foreign leaders, and even fight pirates and slavers.

The US government called on Shadow Squadron when they had an interest in military intervention but couldn't act openly for tactical, political, or legal reasons. The team had succeeded in nearly every mission, which was a major point of pride for Lieutenant Commander Cross.

"Morning," Cross said. He began to swipe through icons on the touchpad as Walker ceded the position and took a seat. When Cross tapped the one he wanted, a blank teleconferencing window popped up on the whiteboard. "New mission for us today, and Command says to give it top priority. The CIA's Special Activities Division has identified a high-value Al-Qaeda target operating in Yemen. We're going to go and pick him up."

Cross saw questions rising to his soldiers' lips. Rather than answer them all, he tapped the desk touchpad once more to open the teleconference connection. A familiar face appeared. It belonged to a smiling, middle-aged white man with slicked-back hair, a cleft chin, and sporting John Lennon glasses. The corner of his mouth curled up like he was smirking at the camera. Or directly at Cross.

"Ryan, good morning!" the man said, as if greeting an old friend after a long absence.

"Agent Upton," Cross replied with a nod. He glanced up at his team to gauge their reactions.

Agent Bradley Upton was a longtime Central Intelligence Agency field operative who worked in secret around the world, fighting the war on terror. Working hand-in-glove with the JSOC, Upton helped find the secret places where terrorists armed themselves and executed their plans. His mission was to foil their plans and bring them to justice. His primary centre of operations had been Iraq for many years, but since US forces had largely left that country, Upton had transitioned to Yemen.

The CIA operative did most of his work alone, but he coordinated the efforts of several other divisions. Like Shadow Squadron, those teams performed high-risk black ops. The day Cross had been offered leadership of Shadow Squadron, Upton tried to steal him for his own team. Upton had offered greater glory, more operational freedom, and much more money than the Shadow Squadron position offered. Fortunately, Cross had previously worked with Upton and knew what kind of man he really was. That was to say, not a good one.

The rest of Shadow Squadron had got to know Upton during their last mission in Iraq. Through favour-trading above Cross's rank, Upton "borrowed" Cross's team for use as bodyguards for an Iraqi CIA informant. The informant had turned out to be a former terrorist who sold information about his former allies in exchange for money, prestige, and political power. He'd also proven himself a coward who'd tried to use his ten-year-old grandson as a sniper shield when assassins had come for him.

The fact that Agent Upton had placed such value on the informant's life earned the team's scorn. Cross understood their hostility toward Upton.

Only one person in the room didn't know Upton as anything other than a name on old files. "And this must be Miss Lancaster," the agent said.

"It's Staff Sergeant Lancaster," Chief Walker said with a scowl.

Staff Sergeant Morgan Lancaster looked to the whiteboard and gave a cool nod. The most recent addition to Shadow Squadron, Lancaster was one of the first women to enter and graduate from the Air

Force Combat Control School. If she took the same offence to Upton's comment that Chief Walker had, she showed no sign of it.

"Staff Sergeant Lancaster," Upton said through an overly sweet smile. "I've read a lot of good things about you. Welcome to the team."

"We're just starting the briefing, Agent Upton," Cross said. "The intel on our target all comes from you. Would you like to do the honours?"

"After you," Upton said. "I'll correct you if you get anything wrong." He smiled again. "Not that I expect you to. You've been very well informed."

Cross didn't like the look of Upton's eyes. Behind his John Lennon specs, Upton seemed distant and calculating. No matter how much he smiled and complimented others, no hint of warmth flickered in those cold eyes.

Cross tapped the touchpad once more. A second window appeared beside Upton's, showing a satellite map of the Arabian Peninsula. Cross highlighted Yemen, the country on the peninsula's southwestern corner. As the image appeared on the whiteboard,

Cross glanced up at Second Lieutenant Aram Jannati at the far end of the table. Jannati was the youngest and second-newest member of Shadow Squadron. According to Jannati's file, his grandfather had immigrated to America from Yemen in the early 1960s. Surprisingly, the location of the mission hadn't seemed to affect the young soldier.

In a third window, Cross produced a cropped photo showing a man wearing a long grey robe, a crocheted taqiyah cap, and pince-nez spectacles. The man had a scraggly beard and very little hair under his cap. In the photo, he was smiling at something off camera.

"This is our target," the Commander said. "We've never learned his real name or country of origin, but his known associates all call him Ustadh. Word has it he's one of Al-Qaeda's most talented and dangerous bomb makers. He spent most of the war years moving around Iraq teaching the insurgents how to build and plant IEDs, car bombs, and explosive belts. Hence the name."

"Ustadh means 'the professor' in Arabic," Upton chimed in.

"He's slippery, this one," Cross added, "and one I've got some personal experience with. My old SEAL team actually went after him a few times, but he was always one step ahead of us. Last we heard, he'd died in Baqubah with Abu Musab Al-Zarqawi in 2006."

"That was my mistake, as Ryan seems too polite to say," Agent Upton said. "My people provided that inaccurate report."

"Apparently," Cross said, "one of Zarqawi's lieutenants was misidentified as Ustadh. As soon as we thought he was dead, the Professor fled the country with no one looking for him. Now that he's popped up in Yemen, evidence suggests he's looking to hook up with AQAP."

The terrorist organization known as Al-Qaeda in the Arabian Peninsula (or AQAP) had grown out of the original Al-Qaeda Islamist militant group founded by the late Osama bin Laden. It had perpetrated a sickeningly long list of bombings and other attacks against Yemeni, Saudi, and American targets. Intel suggested they planned to do far worse in the coming months.

"How solid is this lead?" Chief Walker asked, not bothering to conceal the skepticism in his voice. He'd been frowning since the briefing started — and with good reason. Normally Cross discussed mission plans with him before the two of them brought the specifics to the rest of the team. However, Cross hadn't been able to do so this time around because the arrangement with Upton had been last-minute.

Additionally, Command asked Cross to keep certain information to himself on this mission. Chief Walker didn't like surprises or secrets, especially when they came from higher up the chain of command.

"I wouldn't say I trust the source," Cross said, "but I believe his information is legit."

From his teleconference window on the whiteboard, Upton laughed. No one else joined in.

"I have a question," Staff Sergeant Adam Paxton said from near the back of the room. The former Green Beret looked at Cross, but it was Upton who answered. "Ask away, Adam."

Paxton waited for Cross to nod his permission then looked directly into the tiny camera's eye.

"Why are you coming to us with this?" Paxton asked. "We've got special forces all over Yemen and the rest of the Middle East these days."

"You've got people of your own too," Sergeant Mark Shepherd added. "You had half a platoon with you in our mission in Nasiriyah."

"That was Nasiriyah," Upton said. "I've only been in Yemen a little while. All the same, when we stumbled over Ustadh here, my first thoughts were of your commander. I know how important capturing the Professor is to him. I owe him a chance to be the one to bring him in. It was one of my junior agents who misidentified Ustadh as K.I.A. with Zarqawi in 2006. Thus, letting him get away was my responsibility, and now I've got a chance to make that right. Even if that were all there is to it, that would still be plenty enough for me."

"This bomb maker has escaped from me three different times," Cross said, addressing his soldiers. "The first time, he made me look like the green idiot I was. The second time, he laid a trap in what we thought was his safe house. Three Navy SEALs died that day. And this last escape was the worst because it was caused by plain human error. He's been laughing behind my back for almost a decade, and I'm sick of it. Agent Upton's got the goods on this guy, so we're going to bring him down once and for all. Ustadh isn't getting away from me again."

He paused and took a deep breath. It wasn't like him to make a mission personal, and his team knew that. Time to dial it back a little.

Fortunately, Jannati spoke first. "We'll get it done, sir," he said.

"Hoo-rah," the rest of the team echoed.

"Ha!" Upton crowed. "Hoo-rah . . ." He said the word like it tasted sweet. "That's what I like to hear. And to that end, we believe we know where Ustadh is going to be most vulnerable."

"Where?" Cross asked. For all his big promises, Upton had been stingy with concrete details.

"Well, before I answer that," Upton said, feigning embarrassment, "I need to tell you about a recent development on my end. It's not something I'd normally mention, but it does seem to upset you when I don't tell you every little thing right up front."

"What's happened?" Cross said.

Upton shrugged. "There's a slim possibility that the Professor spotted one of my local guys tailing him yesterday morning. There's no indication yet that he knows who we are, but he knows somebody's watching him now. Worse, he disappeared for half the day after that, and we didn't reacquire him until just about an hour after dinner last night. He's back under surveillance, but all the same . . ."

"At least you didn't lose him," Walker grumbled.

"Again," Upton corrected. "At least I didn't lose him again, you mean. But yes, while we didn't have eyes on him, he could have been making arrangements to disappear on us. Frankly, for all we know, he could have been building a suitcase nuke. We don't know what he was doing, and I don't like that. I'd like to accelerate the timetable and make a move on the target sooner rather than later. I'm sure Ryan agrees."

"I do," Cross said.

"And what do you get out of this, Agent Upton?" Yamashita asked. His voice was steady and his face was a neutral mask. Cross, however, knew his sniper well enough to read his eyes. He was burning with contempt for Upton, the man's methods, and the company he kept in the name of doing business.

Upton winked. "It's not nothing," he admitted. "Nothing in this life is free."

Cross knew that Upton would expect something in exchange for the opportunity he offered. The fact that Upton hadn't wanted to discuss it until Cross was on the spot in front of his men implied it would be something big.

"The Professor is having a meeting with a suspected AQAP financier Wednesday afternoon at 1:00 PM local time at a historical site in Aden called the Tawila Cisterns. He's cagey on the phone and in his emails, but we think he has been trying to lure the Professor out of retirement for something big that AQAP has planned. Ustadh has been reluctant to draw attention to himself since his reported death, but he's agreed to the meeting anyway."

Cross braced himself. "What do you want?" he ordered.

"What I want," Upton said, "is to have a talk with that financier. I think there's plenty about Al-Qaeda he can tell us. So, your job is going to be to capture him alive and hand him over to me. You do that, and the Professor is all yours."

That price isn't as high as I expected, Cross thought. "We might be able to do that. I wonder, though, what's keeping JSOC from just sending a team that's already in country to get Ustadh right now, seeing as to how you've already got him under surveillance."

"What's keeping JSOC — and you — from doing so is that you don't know where he's under surveillance. My people are the only ones who do, and I decide who I share that information with," Upton said. "All the same, trust me when I say that Ustadh is too well guarded to just grab. Not that your men aren't talented, Ryan, but he'd know you were coming a mile away."

"Plus, even if we did just grab him," Walker said,

"this financier you want so badly would vanish as soon as we did."

"You get a gold star, Chief Walker," Upton said. "That's exactly why you can't have Ustadh until I get my financier. Oh, and just so we're clear, information is our mission priority here. If something should happen to my target or if he should get away, I'll be more than happy to settle for your Professor instead and see what he can tell me under interrogation."

"You're assuming they won't die while resisting capture," Cross said.

"Oh, I have every confidence you won't let that happen," Upton said. "I hate to think how the relationship between our two organizations might be damaged if that ended up being the case. Especially after I brought you into this as a personal favour."

"You'll have nothing to worry about," Cross assured him, though he hated the taste of every word he'd spoken. "As for the operation itself, we'll need to unify command of our two teams in the field. How many SOG guys do you have at your disposal these days?"

"Well, about that," Upton said, feigning embarrassment. "I'm a little short-handed just now. Special Activities hasn't put a full SOG team at my disposal here like the one I had in Iraq. I've got an analyst and a junior agent or two I can call, but when it comes to the physical side, I'm short."

"So that's why you called on us," Walker said, not sounding at all surprised.

"In my defence," Upton said, "yours was the first team I thought of."

Cross sighed. Upton hadn't changed a bit. "All right. Give us everything you've got on Ustadh and whatever you know about this financier, so we know who we're looking for. Anything you can give us on the meeting site — these Tawila Cisterns — would be appreciated as well."

"I can do that," Upton said. "I've got it all right here."

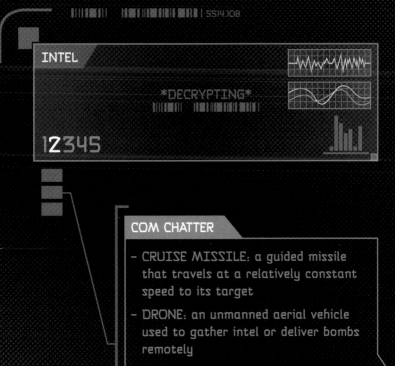

INTEL

DECRYPTING

12345

COM CHATTER

- CRUISE MISSILE: a guided missile that travels at a relatively constant speed to its target
- DRONE: an unmanned aerial vehicle used to gather intel or deliver bombs remotely
- UAV: unmanned aerial vehicle, also known as a drone
- M110 SNIPER RIFLE: a semi-automatic sniper rifle

3245.98 ● ● ●

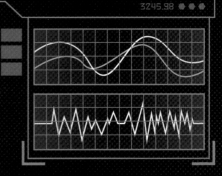

THE FINANCIER

Somewhere in Yemen — Now . . .

"Ryan, think about this," Upton said, his voice rising slightly.

Cross stared at the gun on the coffee table for a long moment. If he leaned forward against the ropes around his legs, he could just reach the weapon with his right hand. Instead, he reached across his body and used his bound left hand to scratch a powerful itch in his right forearm.

"Indeed, think about it," said the nightmare named Ustadh. "You could live a hero or die a self-righteous fool."

"Killing a beaten-up man just so I can live doesn't sound very heroic," Cross said. "Besides, how do I know you won't just kill me anyway when I shoot him?"

"What do you mean 'when'?" Upton chirped.

Cross ignored Upton. "And am I really supposed to believe you'd give me a chance to shoot you instead of him?" Cross continued.

"This is a test of honour," Ustadh said. He spread his hands out as if inviting Cross to shoot him. "Mine no less than yours."

"I can't help but notice that I get shot either way," Upton pointed out.

"You have no honour!" Ustadh snapped at him. "You're a monster! Monsters deserve to die!"

Upton flinched and pressed back against the couch. Ustadh closed his eyes and took a deep, calming breath.

"What's this now?" Cross asked, raising a sore eyebrow. "How is Upton more a monster than you are?"

"I am just a technician," Ustadh replied. "I make devices and teach the making of such devices. What others do with those devices is not my concern. I make no secret of what my devices are capable of, but they choose to use them anyway. Those others' choices do not make me a monster."

It was as flawed an argument as Cross had ever heard, but he wasn't in a position to debate morality at the moment. "But Upton is a monster?" Cross asked.

"Oh, my," Ustadh said, genuinely surprised. "Do you know what this man does?"

"He hunts terrorists," Cross said.

"Yes," Ustadh said. "And when he finds one, he tells someone like you. And someone like you targets your robotic drones or your cruise missiles at the terrorist. And your missiles fly or your bombs fall. And innocent people die."

"That's warfare, Professor," Upton growled. "If you don't like it then stay out of the business."

"It would be warfare," Ustadh said, "if your

enemies were the only ones who died." He spoke slowly, biting off every word in an attempt to keep his anger in check. Cross saw Ustadh's fingers curl into fists as if he were going to lash out and crack Upton across the face.

"But that is not how you operate," Ustadh said. "You don't care who dies when your missiles fly and your bombs fall. You don't care whether innocents die — wives, even children! You don't care as long as your targets perish along with them. Do you?"

Upton looked Ustadh in the eye for a second, as if searching for some clever response. But no words passed his lips. He looked away, bringing a triumphant smile to Ustadh's face.

"What are you trying to say?" Cross asked. "Are you telling me he's knowingly called down drone strikes on civilian targets?"

"That is exactly what I'm saying," Ustadh said. "He did it in Iraq many times. He has even committed this same crime here in Yemen, no doubt."

"I have plenty of doubt," Cross said. "Where's your proof?"

"It's true," Upton said. "Not the Yemen bit, but everything else. I've targeted civilian centres where scumbag terrorists were hiding. But those scumbags are the ones putting the civilians in danger, not me. They're taking their own people hostage, thinking they don't have to face justice for their crimes. Well, they're wrong and I've been proving it to them. I've been showing them their actions have consequences. I've been letting them know they can't hide forever."

"He even admits it," Ustadh said. He turned to Cross. "From his own lips, he names himself a war criminal. His tone makes him sound proud of his actions. Is such a man truly worthy of the breath God gave him?"

"That was quite an admission," Cross said slowly.

"You see why he must die," Ustadh said. "It is your duty."

"And then what?" Cross asked. "What's to stop someone else just as bad from doing what Upton's done . . . or worse?"

"You are," Ustadh said, his eyes wide. "Take the gun. Shoot him. Show the others that actions have consequences. Let them know they can't hide forever."

* * *

Two Days Before, in Aden, Yemen . . .

Upton's early reconnaissance footage made the Tawila Cisterns out to be often empty and rarely visited. But on the day of Ustadh's meeting with the AQAP financier, the place was packed. A French tour group had chosen to visit the cisterns that day. They snapped photos with their mobile phones and loitered all over the grounds. Their presence (and the handful of locals in attendance) made it easier for Cross and his team to blend into the scenery without drawing attention.

However, the idea of something going wrong and gunfire breaking out made Cross feel sick to his stomach. Precautions would need to be taken to protect the civilians.

Thankfully, Lancaster was in the team's armoured van down in the car park with Chief Walker and Agent Upton. She was keeping an eye on things via Four-Eyes, the small recon and surveillance UAV quad-copter. "I see Ustadh," Lancaster said through Cross's canalphone. "He's just coming in now. Blue thawb, red-and-white cap."

The Cisterns of Tawila's original purpose was to collect and store rainwater runoff from the mountains and to protect the city below them from flooding. However, construction farther upstream had redirected water flow so that the cisterns were no longer necessary. The only use the site had now was as a tourist attraction.

Cross acknowledged Lancaster's report by tapping his canalphone twice. He looked toward the attraction's entrance and idly scratched his right arm. Ustadh was the only one coming in at the moment. He paused to chat in a friendly fashion with the young woman taking admission tickets at the front gate.

Cross and Hospital Corpsman Second Class Kyle Williams were at the lowest level of the cisterns, spread out among a handful of areas, keeping eyes in all directions. After Lancaster's signal, they'd melted into the afternoon shadows to watch Ustadh unobserved.

All the members of the team wore civilian clothes and were armed only with silenced SIG P226 pistols. Beneath their clothes they wore ultralight spider silk and carbon-fibre ballistic vests, which fitted as closely as a shirt but could stop small arms and light rifle fire. The only exception was Yamashita on Overwatch. The sniper had arrived the previous night after the cisterns had closed down, then climbed high into the surrounding cliffs with his M110 sniper rifle. The hiding spot he'd chosen gave him line of sight on the entire complex, including the car park below.

Ustadh drifted up past the first level of the cisterns to the second. "I see him," Yamashita reported.

"He's coming your way, Paxton," Cross murmured via his canalphone.

"Sir," Paxton replied just as quietly from the middle level where he and Shepherd were keeping watch.

The pair of them were playing the part of Western tourists, chattering about what they were looking at and filming everything in sight with their mobile phones. Their level was the most crowded by the French-speakers in the tour group, so they were forced to circulate and change positions constantly.

When Ustadh paused briefly on one of the ancient bridges to look down toward the city far below, Shepherd had to hand over his camera and ask a couple of lady tourists to take his picture in order to get into a spot within earshot of Ustadh. Shepherd flirted with the tourists in awful French while they giggled and snapped photos of him. The intent was to keep his cover, but he seemed to be enjoying himself.

The target paused on that level for a few minutes then resumed his climb alone. He drew a cigarette and matches from a shiny metal case. Then he climbed to the highest open level of the cisterns. At the top, he lit a cigarette.

"I see him," Jannati said from the top level when Ustadh arrived. Jannati was perched on a bench in the shade and pretending to read a book. A half-empty bottle of water was on the ground beside him. Ustadh took no notice of him.

"I think he just signalled somebody from the stairway," Yamashita said. "This could be it."

"I didn't see a signal," Lancaster said.

"He was turning his mirrored cigarette case in the sun, reflecting it back down the steps," Yamashita said.

Cross paused near the stairway. "Is anybody with him?" Cross murmured.

Jannati double-tapped his canalphone, paused, then did it again. *Negative.*

"Possible contact," Yamashita said. "On the stairway."

"Got him," Lancaster confirmed. "He came in with that big group at two o'clock. Straw hat, cargo shorts. Can't see his face yet."

"Get Four-Eyes down in position where you can," Cross said. "We'll need a shot for Upton."

"I'm trying, sir," Lancaster said, "but something's wrong with Four-Eyes. It's not respond—"

KA-BOOOOM!

A thundering roar shook the Tawila Cisterns. Adrenaline whip-cracked through Cross's system. His hand was already going for his pistol before he fully realized what was going on. The tourists in his field of vision were frozen in place, though only for the moment.

"Car park!" Yamashita said. "IED! IED!" His voice sounded far away in Cross's ringing ears.

Cross spun and took a few steps back in that direction just in time to see a plume of black smoke rising from below. Through a bloom of dust and smoke, he could just make out a scorched, blackened ruin where the French tourists' bus had been. The next nearest vehicle to it, Shadow Squadron's van, lay on its side, leaking fluid. The vehicle's unique armour and construction had kept it from being blown apart, but it had been parked right next to the bus. Were Lancaster, Walker, and Upton still alive? Could they have survived that?

Instead of an answer, chaos came Cross's way. The girl who'd been taking admissions at the foot of the stairway saw the bus. Her scream awoke animal-like terror in the onlookers.

"They're trying to kill us!" someone shouted.

"Go up!" another person cried.

"There could be more bombs! There's never just one!"

"Go down!"

"Get out of the way!"

"Walker!" Cross shouted over the din, battering at his canalphone. "Lancaster! Report!"

"Where's Ustadh?" Yamashita's voice called.

"He was right here!" Jannati answered then let out a loud curse. "I lost him. What's happening down there?"

Cross wished he knew. With the floodgates of panic open, every visitor to the cisterns had suddenly tried to pour down the stairs from the middle level. The lower level was completely jammed. The crowd couldn't decide which way to stampede, so Cross was forced to maintain his position amidst the bubbling cauldron of frightened humanity.

"He's not here!" Jannati cried desperately. "Did he go back down?"

"Man down," Shepherd said, his voice heavy and oddly slurred. "Me. I am that man. Medic . . . ?"

"He's all right," Paxton said. "Crowd knocked him into one of the canals. He'll be fine."

"I'm coming," Williams said. Cross saw the medic shoving his way through the people jammed on the lower-level stairwell.

"Belay that," Cross said. "Get to the van. We could have three—"

Cross never saw what stung him. He'd been fighting his way out of the fear-maddened crowd, trying to catch some glimpse of Ustadh when a wasp-like sting jabbed him in the shoulder. His eyes drooped like heavy stage curtains, and he realized he was collapsing.

Did I get a shot, he wondered. He struggled to focus on something in the haze that clouded his gaze. *I already had an injection,* he thought deliriously. *Shots suck.*

Cross's mind and body floated in disconnected little bubbles, neither one troubling the other. He felt someone standing over him.

Cross tried to crane his neck to look up, but he couldn't. The person dug the canalphone out of Cross's ear and crushed it under his feet.

"Hey, those are expensive," Cross mumbled.

Someone else knelt on the other side of Cross. The two of them reached out and hefted Cross between them.

They shouted in French that their friend needed help and for everyone to clear the way.

The Chief speaks French, too, Cross remembered. *The Chief is awesome. I hope he's okay. Doesn't he have kids . . . ?*

INTEL

DECRYPTING

12345

COM CHATTER

- AL-QAEDA: radical Sunni Muslim organization dedicated to fighting the Western presence in Arab countries

- AK-47: Soviet-designed, gas-operated assault rifle

- GREEN ZONE: a high-security, central area in Baghdad

- INSURGENT: a rebel soldier

3245.98

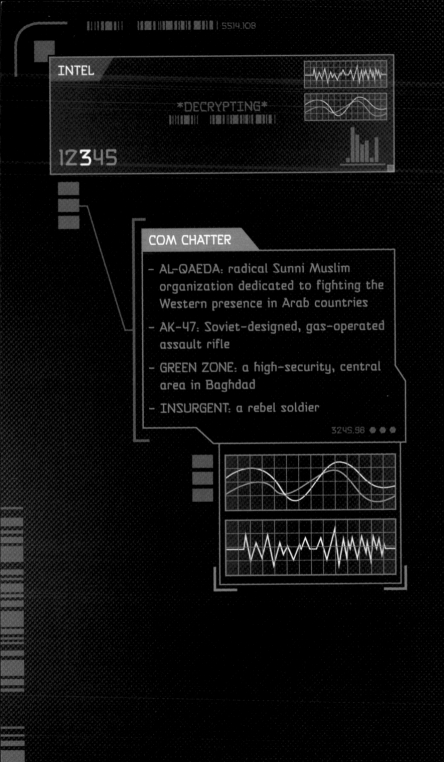

THE INSURGENT

Baqubah, Iraq. Several Years Ago . . .

It grew harder to think of the prisoner as an insurgent the longer Lieutenant Cross sat across the table from him. The more the two of them faced each other, the more Cross thought of him as the boy's father.

Cross's SEAL team had captured the man and his seventeen-year-old son at the end of a raid on an Al-Qaeda weapons depot that morning. The boy had been shot in the shoulder as he hung out a window firing an AK-47 wildly with one hand. Cross was the one who'd shot him. Cross had also been the first one into the room where the boy lay after his team had taken the depot. There he'd found the boy's father trying to bandage the wound. The man had looked at a pistol lying nearby when Cross's SEALs entered, but he'd been outnumbered and outgunned. The fight had left him.

And now here he was, glaring at Cross and refusing to even speak to him except to demand to see his son.

"Your son's being treated," Cross told him again. "As soon as you tell us what we need to know, you'll be reunited. All we want is your cell's supplier. We need to know how you're getting your weapons and who's paying for them."

"Allah provides," the man said sarcastically, his voice dripping with contempt. "We pray and the weapons rain down from Heaven. Every Muslim can do this. Did you not know?"

Cross gritted his teeth. He'd been interrogating the man for hours, and he'd got nowhere. His SEAL team had been tasked with breaking up the flow of weapons into the hands of Al-Qaeda militants operating in Iraq, and discovering this depot had been a major find. Yet for all his efforts, Cross had no new information. He was at his wits' end, and the man across the table from him clearly knew it. Cross was tempted to physically intimidate the man. Instead, he took a deep breath and tried talking again.

"Listen, I don't want to do this all night. If I let you see your son first, would that get you to —"

SLAM!

Before he could finish the sentence, the door behind him banged open. A man Cross had never met came in. He was white and approaching early middle age, a pair of John Lennon specs perched on the end of his nose.

"You're Cross?" the newcomer asked. "I'm Bradley Upton, CIA."

"Agent Upton, it's good to finally meet in person," Cross said. "I take it you're here to take over the interrogation. I haven't been having much luck."

Upton ran a cold, calculating look over Cross then directed it at the insurgent.

"You're Mustafa's father?" the agent asked. He gave Cross a quick glance to tell him to back off. Cross did. "I don't know how to tell you this, sir . . ."

"He's dead?" the man growled. He tensed in his chair, as if preparing to pounce. Cross put his hand on his pistol.

"He isn't dead," Upton said then let out a sigh. "Not yet. His shoulder is badly infected, though. He's feverish. He's dying. Maybe not today, maybe not tomorrow, but it doesn't look good."

"But I . . . I bandaged it," the man said. "I cleaned it. I removed the bullet."

"Yeah, you did," Upton said. "But you're not exactly a doctor, are you?"

The boy's father — the man who'd shown Cross nothing but angry defiance all day long — sagged uncertainly in his chair. "I thought I helped him. I tried to take care of him."

"I know," Upton said. "I'm sure you did everything you could."

"He's going to die? He'll die?" the man asked.

"Well," Upton said, "he certainly could die. Ryan's corpsman's been working on him all night, but there's only so much he can do. The infection is beyond his power to treat."

It took Cross a moment to realize the agent was referring to Pritchard, the corpsman for Cross's SEAL team. The agent had used Cross's first name so casually that Cross hadn't even noticed. He said it like the two of them were old friends or something. Cross assumed Upton had done that to include him in the rapport he was trying to build with the insurgent, but he wished Upton had at least run it by him first.

Regardless, it was the base's surgeons and doctors who'd been treating this man's son, not Cross's medic. What game was Upton playing?

"Is there someone else?" the insurgent asked, his voice thin and distant. "Another doctor?" His eyes had glazed slightly, and he couldn't bring himself to look Upton or Cross in the face anymore.

"There's no time," Upton told him. "Mustafa is dying, and we're a little bit outside the Green Zone. The only hope for him now is to let Ryan's corpsman take off your son's arm."

The insurgent paled. He looked like someone had punched him in the stomach. "Oh, no . . ."

"Problem is," Upton continued, "he won't let us. We can't get near him with the anesthetics to put him under and do the job. We need your help. You have to convince him that there's no other way to save his life. Can you do that? Will he still listen to you?"

The man nodded slowly. "He always does what I tell him. *Eventually.* Mustafa. Mustafa . . ."

The man tried to stand, but Upton held out a hand to stop him. "Wait, where do you think you're going?"

"To my son," the insurgent said, confusion large on his face. "You said —"

"Well, you can't go yet," Upton said. "Isn't there something you're forgetting?"

The man looked at Upton then over at Cross. He was no less confused than a moment ago. "Forgetting what . . . ?"

"Ryan here asked you some questions earlier," Upton said. "Don't you think you'd better answer them?"

Upton put his fists on the tabletop that lay between himself and the insurgent. He leaned down to loom over the man. "I sure think you should answer them." His voice was still completely calm, but his eyes blazed with intensity. Cross's breath caught in his throat, and he wasn't even the one Upton was pressuring.

The insurgent tried to reignite his anger, but he couldn't do it. His words died in his throat, and he slumped, defeated, into his chair. "What do you want to know?" he asked.

This time, when Cross asked questions, the man answered quickly and with no trace of defiance. His face burned with shame, but the insurgent told everything he knew about his cell's operation and its connection to the rest of Al-Qaeda in Iraq.

It wasn't much, but it was a step in the right direction. It supported certain intelligence Upton and Cross had uncovered separately from other sources and suggested a next target for Cross's SEAL team. The man told them everything they asked for and more, and did so in a great rush so that he could try to save his dying son.

When the interview was complete, Upton thanked him sincerely, shook his hand, and wished him luck with his son. The agent then motioned for Cross to join him and crossed the room to leave.

"What about me?" the insurgent asked desperately. "When can I see Mustafa?"

"I have to let my superiors know that you cooperated," Upton said. "They'll send a car over for you in five minutes."

"Thank you," the man said. His eyes welled up on the verge of tears. "Oh, thank you. Thank you."

Upton pulled Cross out into the hallway and closed the door on the man. The two of them walked toward the stairwell at the end of the hall. Through the thick stone walls of the building, they could hear the faint booms of artillery shells going off and the sporadic cracking of gunfire in the city beyond.

"His son's not with my corpsman," Cross said.

"I know," Upton said. He smiled, though the smile didn't wrinkle his eyes the way a real smile would. "I made up that stuff about the kid's arm. Sure turned the dad into a helpful fella, though, didn't it?"

"So he's not really going to lose his arm?" Cross asked.

"Don't see why he should," Upton shrugged. "The kid was barely grazed by the bullet."

Cross flinched. "What?"

"I lied," Upton said flatly. "Whoever shot him barely hit him. Kid was never in any real danger."

"What are you going to do with his father?" Cross blurted out. "He thinks he's going to see his son. I'm guessing that won't happen."

Upton nodded. "Where he's actually going is to the airfield to catch a flight to Guantanamo Bay. Don't worry about it. My people will take care of it. I've got something bigger in mind for the two of us."

Cross's head started to spin. What Upton had done was the cruellest thing he'd ever seen words do to a man, even if it had been undeniably effective. Still, Cross wondered what kind of man could twist a despairing father's heart without even batting an eyelash?

"Interested, Ryan?" Upton said. "If your team's up for it, I can use what he gave us in there to put an op together that'll break Al-Qaeda's supply chain into a thousand pieces. I can even see there's a promotion in it for you if all goes well. That's worth a little white lie between enemies, right?"

"Maybe," Cross murmured, unable to find a

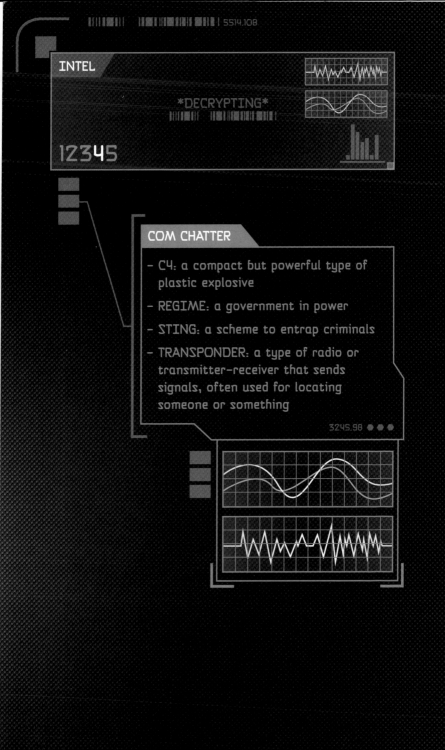

COM CHATTER

- C4: a compact but powerful type of plastic explosive
- REGIME: a government in power
- STING: a scheme to entrap criminals
- TRANSPONDER: a type of radio or transmitter-receiver that sends signals, often used for locating someone or something

3245.98 ● ● ●

CHAPTER FOUR

DARK AGENT

Now, Somewhere in Yemen . . .

"Ryan, say something," Upton urged. It was alarming to hear panic in the voice of a man who always seemed so in control of himself and the situation.

"Yes," Ustadh said, cocking his head and watching Cross intently. "Say something. Or, better yet, *do* something. What is your decision? Will you kill this man?"

"I'm thinking," Cross said slowly, reaching his free right arm to take the pistol off the table. He rested it on his lap and looked at it.

Upton whimpered. "Ryan . . ."

"I'm thinking," Cross said, looking up, "that this whole situation feels . . . staged."

Ustadh's eyes narrowed ever so slightly. That little tell confirmed Cross's suspicions.

"I mean, it's awfully operatic, isn't it, this little stage you've set? And then there's this little dilemma of choosing who lives and who dies." Cross locked eyes with Ustadh. "This obvious irony of a terrorist forcing one American to kill another to punish him for heartless terrorist acts against civilian victims. It's not even operatic. It's melodramatic."

"Don't toy with me," Ustadh said. "Do you think I won't kill you?"

Without a word, Cross pointed the pistol at the ceiling and pulled the trigger. He looked Ustadh in the eye as he did it.

CLICK!

The gun didn't fire. "Bang," Cross said.

Ustadh turned to Upton. "You were right," Ustadh said.

Upton sat up straight on the sofa and smirked at Cross. "I told him you'd see right through it," he said. "That's 5000 rials you owe me, Ustadh."

Amusement coloured Ustadh's face, erasing all trace of the self-righteous terrorist he'd been pretending to be. He shrugged then folded his arms across his chest.

"All right, give us the room," Upton said. "One test is as good as another, I suppose."

Ustadh nodded. He left, closing the door behind him. Upton wriggled and twisted his wrists, loosening the bonds that held his hands together. Once the coils fell slack and dropped on the floor, Upton reached up to his face. He pulled off a layer of latex and fake blood that had made his face look as bruised and abused as Cross's felt.

When Upton was finished, he looked no different than the last time Cross had seen him.

"Sorry I can't do the same for you, Ryan," Upton said.

"That was some test," Cross said. "I assume I passed?"

"You've always shown the cleverness I desire in a soldier," Upton said. "The real issue I wanted to explore was your loyalty. I wanted to know if you could put our friendship in front of the high-minded ideals you military types get drilled into you."

"Friendship?" Cross spat. "Are we friends?"

Upton grinned. "As much as people like us can be, I suppose. You help me get the work done and don't give me a hard time about how I do it. That's rare these days."

"And Ustadh? Is he one of your friends too?"

"He's more like an employee. I saved his life in Baqubah back in 2006 by helping him escape Al-Zarqawi. He's been my little puppy dog ever since."

"And if I'd tried to shoot him?"

"Well, then I would've known for sure you were the man I wanted. As it stands now, however, I've got to figure things out another way." Upton hesitated. "It seems to me you're a straightforward kind of guy. Why don't I just lay it on the table and see what happens?"

"Go ahead," Cross said, struggling to bite back the rage that welled in his chest.

"I'm putting a team together," Upton said. "Top-tier special operators. Smart, capable men who know the value of loyalty but aren't opposed to being handsomely paid for the hard work they do."

"You're trying to rebuild your Special Operations Group?" Cross asked.

"Oh, no. This is a personal operation. All off the record, under the table, answering only to me. This isn't anything the JSOC or the CIA — or anybody else, really — needs to know about. I don't offer health and dental or a retirement package, but the work pays so well you'll never have to worry about any of that stuff."

"What is the work, exactly?" Cross asked.

"It's all about controlling the chaos here in the

Middle East," Upton explained. "We keep right on fighting our little war on terror, just like we have been doing, but more with the mindset of a gardener instead of an exterminator. We keep out the dangerous invasive species — the ultra-radicals and the extremists — but tend and nourish the less dangerous plant life. We keep nukes and bioweapons out of the bad guys' hands, sure, but maybe we turn a blind eye if a rebel group gets its hands on a shipment of rifles or C4. We keep them in check so they don't run rampant, but we don't stomp them out altogether. Not unless they turn their eyes toward America, that is. If they do that, we burn them down and replant."

"I don't see where the money comes from," Cross said. Keeping his voice calm was no easy feat. What Upton was saying made Cross want to vomit.

"Congress," Upton said. "Those guys pay through the nose in foreign aid money to keep terrorist threats bottled up in faraway countries like this one. If a foreign government calls itself a US ally in the war on terror and looks like it's trying hard to fight Al-Qaeda, our government practically throws money at it to help the cause. Not every regime knows how to take advantage of that system, though."

"But you do," Cross said.

Upton nodded. "And for a modest percentage, I can inform certain friends I've made in regimes around the region. I show them how the game is played, then I — *we* — help them tend their gardens."

"You did this in Iraq?" Cross asked.

"Iraq put my kids through college," Upton said. "Ivy League, even."

"Yemen too?" Cross asked.

"Yemen is where you come in," Upton said. "You and anyone else I can get for the team. Al-Qaeda's in bloom here, but we're going to have to work quickly before any other, um . . . gardeners get ahead of us."

"You seem awfully sure I'm already in," Cross said. "I turned you down the last time you tried to recruit me, remember? I joined Shadow Squadron instead."

Upton waved dismissively. "That wasn't a choice. The general put you on the spot at the end of your last tour of duty. I have no doubt whatsoever that if you'd turned him down then he would've found some other pretext to pull you back into the Navy for another four years no matter what I had to say about it."

"Probably," Cross admitted.

"And it's not like I'm trying to make you into one of the bad guys. There are real threats out there that need to be knocked down, and I want you in charge of prioritizing them and taking them out. You can be involved in the other side or the money part as much or as little as you want."

"I'd be lying if I said I wasn't tempted," Cross lied. "But I don't think you're giving me much more of a choice than the general did."

"Worse, actually," Upton confirmed. "But I've got a good read on you, Ryan. One thing you've never been is stupid. You came into the Navy with high ideals, but you've seen how the real world works now. You've seen how evil prospers no matter what so-called 'good men' do about it. You've seen how our government keeps making the same mistakes over and over again, and the world keeps on spiralling out of control. Right now, you're powerless in the face of all that, but I can offer you a better life. With me, you can make a difference. And you can make an obscene amount of money."

Cross grunted. "But if I say no —"

"Then the cover story about what happened to you becomes true," Upton declared. "Right now, your team knows that you and I were kidnapped during a terrorist attack at the Tawila Cisterns. For all they know, extremists murdered us. In a few days, they're going to find two bodies that confirm their suspicions. If you turn me down now, only one of those bodies is going to be a fake. And I assure you that this is not melodrama. I like you, Ryan, but I will kill you rather than let you become a liability."

Cross took a deep breath. "I thought I knew you pretty well, Bradley. Up until a few weeks ago, I figured you were just a smug, cynical, self-centred charmer. All the same, I always figured that at least you were on our side. But Command was right about you all along."

A tiny crease appeared over Upton's eyebrows. "Command? What are you talking about?"

"They know," Cross said. "This scam you're so proud of. The one you were running in Iraq. The one you're trying to get started here in Yemen. They know all about it. You've done a brilliant job of hiding it, but this is the twenty-first century. You've laundered money and squirrelled it away in offshore accounts and Swiss banks and fake investments. But as good as you are, we've got people who are better. They figured you out, and now you've played right into their hands."

In truth, Command hadn't foreseen that Upton would use the Yemen operation as an attempt to recruit Cross to his criminal enterprise. *But Upton doesn't need to know that,* Cross thought.

"Originally we were just looking for an opportunity to snatch you up without disrupting CIA operations all across Yemen," Cross went on. "But when you offered up Ustadh, I admit I got greedy. He made for very good bait. All the same, things have worked out so far. Here you are, and here I am."

For the first time in as long as Cross had known him, a genuine smile came to Upton's face. Mirth lit his eyes and he let out a snort. The snort turned into a chuckle. Then the floodgates opened and Upton burst into a teary-eyed guffaw.

"You. Are. *Priceless!*" Upton wheezed, struggling to get himself under control. "This is a sting? This? Well then I guess I surrender! Should I untie you now so you can take me into custody? Or would you like to hit me with that empty gun a few times first?"

Cross smiled back, though it was a sad, pitying one. "Let me show you something . . ."

Without waiting for a reply, Cross used his bound left hand to unbutton his right sleeve's cuff and pulled the sleeve up to his elbow. On the inside of his right forearm was an itchy red welt that had been bothering Cross all week. He turned his arm so Upton could see the mark.

"Command needed to be able to find me in case you got me away from my team," Cross said. "So before we left, our doctor injected a subcutaneous GPS transponder under my skin. Wherever it is you've taken me, my team's already found you. They might not get here in time to stop you from killing me, but you're not going to get away."

As the reality of the situation sank in, the smile faded from Upton's face. He reached into his jacket and produced a matte-black .45 caliber M1911 pistol. He stood and aimed the pistol at Cross's head. "Then I suppose we have nothing more to talk about." He frowned then added with real confusion, "How did I read you so wrong?"

As the last word left Upton's mouth, the lights went out, plunging the room into darkness. Reacting on pure instinct, Cross lifted the empty SIG P226 in his right hand and hurled it where Upton's face had been. Fortunately, Upton proved a split second too slow in the darkness.

THWACK!

Cross's pistol smashed Upton in the face, throwing his aim off.

The bullet nicked Cross alongside his temple, drawing a line of fire above his ear. He hissed in pain, but he knew Upton had got the worst of it. The CIA agent lurched backward and sat down hard on the sofa, dropping his pistol.

"Zahid!" Upton shouted, spitting blood and clutching his nose. "Get in here!" He thumped down off the couch and groped blindly on the floor for his gun.

Whether Zahid was Ustadh's real name or the name of another of Upton's men, Cross didn't know. He heard feet thumping down the hallway outside the door and did the first thing he could think of. With a tremendous heave, he lurched sideways and tipped his chair over onto its right side.

THUD!

Cross came down hard on his shoulder but managed not to pin his arm under his body. Like Upton, he flailed around in search of the dropped M1911.

CRUNCH!

With a thunderous crash, the door came off one hinge and swung into the room by the twisted remains of the other hinge.

"Ha!" Upton crowed at the same moment, finding his pistol and aiming it at Cross.

"Drop it!" someone barked in Midwestern-accented English. "Drop it, Upton!" Lancaster ordered.

He didn't. Two shots rang out in quick succession.

BANG!

BANG!

Then all was silent.

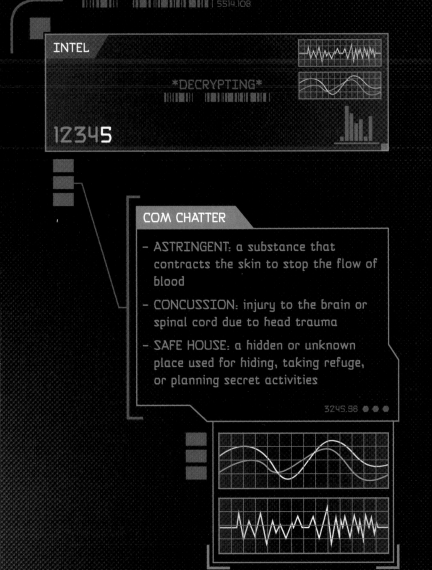

INTEL

DECRYPTING

12345

COM CHATTER

- ASTRINGENT: a substance that contracts the skin to stop the flow of blood
- CONCUSSION: injury to the brain or spinal cord due to head trauma
- SAFE HOUSE: a hidden or unknown place used for hiding, taking refuge, or planning secret activities

3245.98

CHAPTER FIVE

1324.014

PARALYZED

Now, in Qulansiyah, Yemen . . .

Williams dabbed the cut on Cross's temple with something cold and astringent. "Is that where we are?" Cross asked, pointing at Lancaster's touchpad.

"Yes, sir," Lancaster said over Williams' shoulder. "Qulansiyah to be exact. This was Ustadh's safe house, as far as we can tell."

"How are you feeling?" Cross asked. "Last I saw you, you were in the van. When that bus blew up right next to it, I feared the worst."

"I'm fine, sir," Lancaster said. "Got lucky. But the Chief got the worst of it. His hearing's damaged. He might be permanently deaf. We don't know yet. And he's . . . when the van . . ."

"His back's broken," Williams finished for her. "Barring a miracle, he's going to be paralyzed from the waist down."

The news hit Cross like a punch in the gut. Despite being seated, he felt like he was falling.

"Shepherd has a concussion from his fall at the cisterns," Williams went on. "Jannati and Paxton each took a couple of shots in their vests on the way in here, but they're up and about. I need to check on them again once we're done here. Got the wind knocked out of them pretty bad, but the ballistic vests got the job done."

"You're done here," Cross said softly. "Go take care of the others."

Williams frowned but knew better than to refuse. He gathered up his supplies and left the room, sparing a look at Bradley Upton's blanket-covered body in the corner before he left.

"Doesn't feel like a win, does it?" Cross asked Lancaster when they were the only ones left in the room. He couldn't take his eyes off Upton's still form. Lancaster stared as well. Her bullet had taken his life. Upton's own shot had gone into the wall beside her.

"Well," she said, "we did stop him. And we even captured Ustadh. That should feel like a win, shouldn't it?"

Cross shrugged. While the others had finished checking the safe house and rounding up the rest of Upton's men, he told Lancaster about what Upton had wanted from him. Looking at her, Cross could tell she wanted to say something.

After a few moments, Lancaster worked up the courage. "Did he really think he knew you, sir?"

"What?" Cross asked.

"I mean, I don't think I know you all that well," she continued, "but I wouldn't have expected you to turn traitor just for money. Or for any reason, really." She looked at Upton's body. "Did he honestly think that you would?"

Cross sighed. "Maybe he wanted to prove something to himself. Maybe he thought that if he could convince me to get on board with this racket of his, then maybe what he was doing wouldn't seem quite as bad."

"So what did he want? Your approval?"

"Could be."

"Why you?"

Cross grunted. "He liked me. I respected him, and I didn't get on his case about how he did his job. He didn't get that a lot. I think I might have been the closest thing he had to a friend."

"He still tried to kill you."

"Well, I didn't say I was going to miss him," Cross said. He'd meant it to be a joke, but it hadn't come out that way. Instead it sounded flat, hollow, lifeless. The way he felt.

"Sir, about the Chief . . ."

"Not now, Lancaster," Cross said. "I'm not ready to have that conversation yet."

Lancaster nodded. "Well, when you're ready, sir," she said, "we're here."

For now, Cross thought. He glanced at Upton's body, wondering where he was going to find the courage to face Chief Walker.

You're all here now, Cross thought. *But for how long?*

The dead man gave him no answers.

CLASSIFIED

MISSION DEBRIEFING

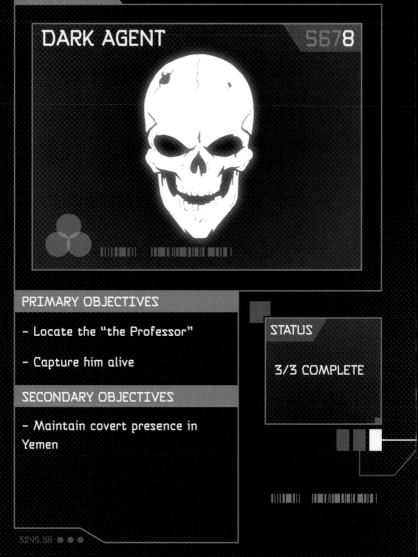

OPERATION

DARK AGENT

5678

PRIMARY OBJECTIVES

- Locate the "the Professor"

- Capture him alive

SECONDARY OBJECTIVES

- Maintain covert presence in Yemen

STATUS

3/3 COMPLETE

3245.98

CROSS, RYAN

RANK: Lieutenant Commander
BRANCH: Navy SEAL
PSYCH PROFILE: Team leader
of Shadow Squadron. Control
oriented and loyal, Cross insisted
on hand-picking each member of
his squad.

I keep telling myself it could've been worse. Everyone made it out alive, we eliminated a terrible bomb maker and exposed a corrupt CIA agent, and you all managed to save my skin . . . but all I can think about right now is the Chief. His unflinching commitment and military expertise are a vital part of Shadow Squadron. I don't want to consider the possibility that we might lose him.

That said, great work out there . . . and thanks again for saving my life.

– Lieutenant Commander Ryan Cross

ERROR
UNAUTHORIZED
USER MUST HAVE LEVEL 12 CLEARANCE
OR HIGHER IN ORDER TO GAIN ACCESS
TO FURTHER MISSION INFORMATION.

2019.681

CREATOR BIO(S)

AUTHOR

CARL BOWEN

Carl Bowen is a father, husband, and writer living in Lawrenceville, Georgia. He was born in Louisiana, lived briefly in England, and was raised in Georgia where he went to school. He has published a handful of novels, short stories, and comics. For Stone Arch Books, he has retold *20,000 Leagues Under the Sea*, *The Strange Case of Dr. Jekyll and Mr. Hyde*, *The Jungle Book*, *Aladdin and the Magic Lamp*, *Julius Caesar*, and *The Murders in the Rue Morgue*. He is the original author of *BMX Breakthrough* as well as the Shadow Squadron series.

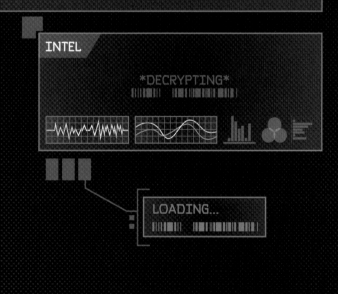

INTEL

DECRYPTING

LOADING...

WILSON TORTOSA

Wilson "Wunan" Tortosa is a Filipino comic book artist best known for his work on *Tomb Raider* and the American relaunch of *Battle of the Planets* for Top Cow Productions. Wilson attended Philippine Cultural High School, then went on to the University of Santo Tomas where he graduated with a Bachelor's Degree in Fine Arts, majoring in Advertising. .

BENNY FUENTES

Benny Fuentes lives in Villahermosa, Tabasco, in Mexico, where the temperature is just as hot as the sauce. He studied graphic design in college, but now he works as a full-time illustrator in the comic book and graphic novel industry for companies like Marvel, DC Comics, and Top Cow Productions. He shares his home with two crazy cats, Chelo and Kitty, who act like they own the place.

2019.681

AUTHOR DEBRIEFING

CARL BOWEN

Q/When and why did you decide to become a writer?
A/I've enjoyed writing ever since I was in elementary school. I wrote as much as I could, hoping to become the next Lloyd Alexander or Stephen King, but I didn't sell my first story until I was in college. It had been a long wait, but the day I saw my story in print was one of the best days of my life.

Q/What made you decide to write *Shadow Squadron*?
A/As a kid, my heroes were always brave knights or noble loners who fought because it was their duty, not for fame or glory. I think the special ops soldiers of the US military embody those ideals. Their jobs are difficult and often thankless, so I wanted to show how cool their jobs are and also express my gratitude for our brave warriors.

Q/What inspires you to write?
A/My biggest inspiration is my family. My wife's love and support lifts me up when this job seems too hard to keep going. My son is another big inspiration.

He's three years old, and I want him to read my books and feel the same way I did when I read my favourite books as a kid. And if he happens to grow up to become an elite soldier in the US military, that would be pretty awesome, too.

Q/Describe what it was like to write these books.
A/The only military experience I have is a year I spent in the Army ROTC. It gave me a great respect for the military and its soldiers, but I quickly realized I would have made a pretty awful soldier. I recently got to test out a friend's arsenal of firearms, including a combat shotgun, an AR-15 rifle, and a Barrett M82 sniper rifle. We got to blow apart an old fax machine.

Q/What is your favourite book, movie, and game?
A/My favourite book of all time is *Don Quixote*. It's crazy and it makes me laugh. My favourite movie is either *Casablanca* or *Double Indemnity*, old black-and-white movies made before I was born. My favourite game, hands down, is *Skyrim*, in which you play a heroic dragonslayer. But not even *Skyrim* can keep me from writing more *Shadow Squadron* stories, so you won't have to wait long to read more about Ryan Cross and his team. That's a promise.

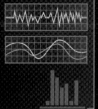

INTEL

DECRYPTING

5678

COM CHATTER

-MISSION PREVIEW: Shadow Squadron welcomes their first female team member, then Cross receives an urgent call from a powerful senator. He demands the team aid in saving his kidnapped son. When the team touches down in Mali, they learn that something far more sinister than kidnapping is going on in the desert . . .

3245.98 ● ● ●

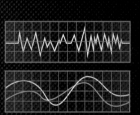

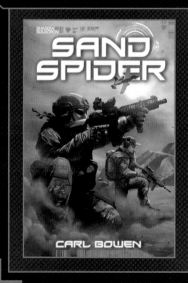

SHADOW SQUADRON

SAND SPIDER

CARL BOWEN

1324.014

SAND SPIDER

The sun had set when Bugaba's men set out for their intended retaliation against Cadran Solaire. The new moon sky glowed with a dusting of countless stars, and the sound of engines carried for miles through the darkness.

"They're coming, Commander," Lancaster said through her canalphone. From her vantage at Overwatch, Lancaster was watching the road through the camera of the remote-controlled "Four-Eyes" quad-copter that Edgar Brighton had built.

Cross lay in the dirt at Attack One a few yards away from the Growler manned by Aram Jannati.

His M4 carbine was propped on his half-empty backpack. His AN/PSQ-20 nightvision lens painted the ambush point in shades of bright green. "How many?" Cross asked.

"Five full Jeeps, one man each on the .50 cals," Lancaster reported. "There's an ACMAT truck behind them. It has a large cage on the back."

"Is it empty?" Cross asked.

"Yes, sir."

"Noted," Cross said. "Seems Bubaga intends to bring any survivors back to his base as slaves."

"That ACMAT could work to block the road behind the Jeeps," Yamashita said over the channel.

"Make it happen when we drop the roadblock in front," Cross said. "Cover One, move to Cover Two."

"Sir," Paxton replied. A moment later, he reported that he was at his new position.

Another few minutes after that, Lancaster reported that the Jeeps were right around the corner. Cross ordered his soldiers to get ready. The engine noise was right on top of them, and the Jeeps' headlights

shone from around the blind corner. Cross lifted his nightvision lens so the headlights wouldn't blind him. "Contact. Roadblock ready."

"Ready, sir," Lancaster said.

The first Jeep's headlights passed right under the high sandstone shelf where Cross and Jannati's Growler was perched. No one in the Jeep seemed to notice them waiting up there. Nor did they spot Attack Two ahead. Two more Jeeps rounded the corner. Then two more. The ACMAT came last.

"Close the road," Cross said.

"Sir," Lancaster said.

Cross looked away as the C4 plastic explosive, placed in the high rock wall beside the road ahead of the Jeeps, exploded. The night shook with a heavy boom. Rocks the size of barrels tumbled into the road. A cloud of dust billowed out in all directions.

A second later, a muted crack sounded at the rear of the slaver convoy. Cross saw the windscreen of the ACMAT shatter inward as Yamashita eliminated the driver with a silenced shot from his M110 sniper rifle. The truck nosed toward the edge of the road and coasted to a stop, blocking the way out. The five Jeeps were now trapped between it and the rockslide.

"Attack One, Attack Two," Cross said. "Go."

Jannati and Shepherd opened up with the Growler's guns, cutting into the first and last vehicles in the line. Jannati targeted the ACMAT's hood with a laser-accurate stream of 7.62x55mm NATO rounds from the minigun, blowing the engine to smithereens so no one could drive away. From farther up, Shepherd sprayed a second stream into the lead Jeep. The driver of that vehicle slammed on his brakes as Shepherd's bullets tore into the side of the vehicle and sent gouts of black smoke pouring from under its bonnet.

The Jeeps left in the middle lurched to a stop, and the men within reacted in a semi-coordinated panic. The second one backed up a few feet and made as if to try to manoeuver around the smoking hulk of the first Jeep. Its headlights washed directly over Attack Two, illuminating Shepherd at the M134 and Walker in a shooter's crouch behind a rock. The third Jeep

backed into the fourth, which was trying to move around to follow the second. The man at the fourth Jeep's machine gun fell off, and the third Jeep's gunner fired a burst in the air as he clung to the weapon for balance. The fifth Jeep remained where it was, and the men inside leaped out to return fire.

"Flares!" Cross called over the din.

"Sir!" Lancaster called over the canalphone.

A second later, a set of magnesium lights lit up the desert night. The flares had been Lancaster's idea. Hidden on the road all along the ambush site and detonated by remote, they blazed to furious life among the startled would-be raiders. At such close quarters, the near light blinded the Malians and made their distant targets nearly impossible to see. From outside the immediate area of effect, the light illuminated the Malians perfectly, making them better targets.

"Fire at will," Cross said quietly.

BANG BANG BANG BANG BANG BANG BANG BANG BANG BANG BANG BANG BANG

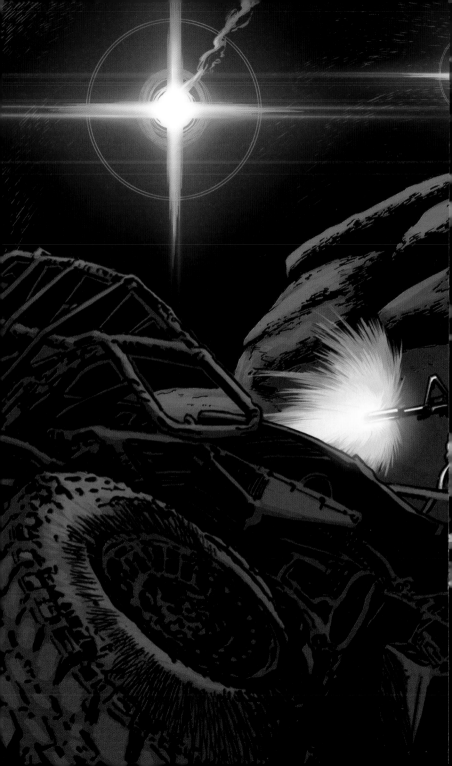

Thunder shattered the night. Walker shot down the machine gunner on the destroyed lead Jeep. The gunner on the fifth Jeep tried to return fire on Attack One through the magnesium glare. Most of his shots were wide to the left, but Cross heard a few dig into the Growler's rear end. Jannati turned the M134 on him, cutting him down and shredding the vehicle. Those of the Jeep's occupants who'd made it out threw themselves flat, scrambling for cover behind the other vehicles.

Of the two Jeeps that had collided, only one gunner remained in position, and he swivelled his barrel up toward Attack One. The gunner of the Jeep facing Attack Two opened up, spraying wildly. Some of the bullets tore into Walker's cover, forcing the Chief to dive back out of the way cursing in Spanish. Fire from Shepherd's minigun knocked the shooter from the back of the Jeep.

Cross picked off the gunner between the two collided vehicles while Jannati fired on the rearmost of the two Jeeps to keep the gunner who'd fallen off from trying to reclaim his firing position. The gunner retreated toward what minimal cover he could find.

Most of the passengers of the two collided Jeeps made it out unharmed, though a burst from Paxton's M4 from Cover Two caught the last one out before he could close the door.

"Frag out!" Williams called as Paxton's man slid to the ground, clinging weakly to the door of the Jeep. The corpsman hurled an M67 fragmentation grenade into the space between the rear bumper and grill of the two collided Jeeps. The blast made the vehicles jump apart and threw a hail of deadly steel fragments into the slavers hiding behind them.

"Suppressing fire," Cross ordered. "Attack Two, move down to flank."

"Sir," Walker replied.

As heavy fire from both miniguns worried at the savaged Jeeps like starving wolves, Cross and Walker came down to road level from their cover positions at opposite ends of the ambush site. Cross came down behind the disabled ACMAT truck and put it between himself and his men. Walker came down along the inside of the fallen-stone roadblock and took cover behind the first Jeep. The magnesium flares were still burning, but thick smoke from the vehicles and brownish dust from the C4 explosion hung in the air, reducing visibility. Cross lifted his M4 to the ready and began to make his way forward.

"Oh, right, right," Lancaster said in Cross's canalphone, likely at some silent urging from Yamashita. "Sir, you've got . . . it looks like . . . seven left moving down there."

No sooner were the words out of Lancaster's mouth than the passenger door of the half destroyed Jeep nearest Cross fell off and a half-dead Malian lurched out with a bullpup FAMAS rifle clutched under one bleeding arm. His weapon was already trained on Cross as Cross dropped to one knee to take aim.

POP!

Yet, Yamashita was faster than them both. The sniper's bullet caught the man in the chest, dropping him at Cross's feet.

"Thanks," Cross said.

"Sir," Yamashita said.

"Make that eight," Lancaster said. "Well, now it's seven."

Cross smirked.